Taylor Swift - The Biography

The Taylor Swift Story

Stellar Stories

Contents

Chapter One

A Star Is Born

There are few whose rise to stardom is as meteoric as Taylor Swift's. From a young age, it was clear that she was destined for greatness.

Swift's musical journey began in her small town childhood, where she discovered her love for singing and songwriting. With her guitar in hand, she would spend countless hours honing her craft, practicing chords and experimenting with melodies. It was during these early years that the seeds of her future success were planted.

As a teenager, Swift's passion and talent propelled her to the forefront of the country music scene. Inspired by the likes of Shania Twain and Dixie Chicks, she began performing at local venues, talent shows, and fairs, gaining experience and building a loyal following. Her distinctively honest and relatable lyrics resonated with listeners, who connected with her vulnerability and authenticity.

Swift's breakthrough came in 2006 with the release of her self-titled debut album. Filled with beautifully crafted country-pop songs, it showcased her storytelling abilities and the emotional depth of her songwriting. Tracks like "Tim McGraw," a bittersweet ode to first love, and "Teardrops on My Guitar," capturing the heartache of unrequited love, allowed fans to glimpse into her heart. Meanwhile, up-tempo songs like "Our Song" displayed her infectious energy and optimism.

The success of her debut album served as a launchpad for Swift's career, but it was her sophomore album, "Fearless," released in 2008, that truly solidified her status as a rising star. "Fearless" quickly became a phenomenon, breaking numerous records and topping charts worldwide. With its irresistible blend of country and pop, the album showcased Swift's growth as an artist and songwriter.

"Fearless" not only resonated with her existing fan base, but it also attracted a wider demographic. Swift's ability to capture the essence of teenage experiences, particularly the ups and downs of love, struck a chord with listeners of all ages. The album's crossover success propelled her into mainstream popularity, earning her numerous accolades, including four Grammy Awards, including Album of the Year.

Building on the success of "Fearless," Swift continued to push boundaries with each subsequent album. "Speak Now" (2010) showcased her evolution as a lyricist as she took full control of her storytelling and writing process. The album delved deeper into Swift's personal experiences and emotions, demonstrating her maturity as both an artist and a young woman navigating fame.

In 2012, Swift's transition to pop music with her album "Red" marked another milestone in her career. Collaborating with acclaimed producers and songwriters, she embraced a more expansive sound, experimenting with different genres while still keeping her trademark vulnerability intact. The album's lead single, "We Are Never Ever Getting Back Together," became a chart-topping hit, solidifying Swift as a pop juggernaut.

Four years later, Swift released "1989," a pop-infused masterpiece that was met with critical acclaim and commercial success. Departing from her country roots entirely, she fully embraced the synth-pop sound of the 1980s, crafting an album filled with infectious hooks and anthemic choruses. "1989" propelled Swift to new heights, earning her seven Grammy Awards and making her the first woman to win Album of the Year twice.

Beyond her musical accomplishments, Swift's unwavering dedication to her fans has set her apart. She actively engages with her Swifties through social media, surprise meet-and-greets, and even secret listening parties at her homes. Her connection with her fans is unmatched, and her ability to make individuals feel seen and heard has endeared her to millions worldwide.

But Swift's impact extends far beyond the realm of music. She uses her platform to advocate for causes she believes in, from education and disaster relief to LGBTQ+ rights and feminism. Her philanthropic efforts have earned her respect and admiration not just from her fans, but from various organizations and communities as well.

While Swift's journey has not been without its challenges, she has faced them with grace and resilience. The media's scrutiny and sensationalism have often painted her in an unfavorable light, but she has consistently risen above the noise, emerging stronger and more determined than ever. Through it all, her honesty and transparency have served as a beacon of authenticity in an industry often plagued by artifice.

Chapter Two

A Small Town Childhood

Taylor's journey began in the picturesque town of Wyomissing, Pennsylvania. Born on December 13, 1989, Taylor Alison Swift grew up in a close-knit community, where she developed her love for music and storytelling.

From a young age, it was clear that Swift possessed a special gift for music. Her parents recognized her talent and nurtured her passion by providing her with guitar lessons at the tender age of 10. Swift quickly mastered the instrument, spending countless hours practicing and honing her skills. The guitar became an extension of herself, a vehicle through which she could express her deepest emotions and connect with others.

Wyomissing, with its serene beauty, provided a whimsical backdrop for Swift's imagination to flourish. The town's quaint charm, lined with tree-lined streets and historic buildings, served as a constant source of inspiration for her storytelling. Whether she was strolling through the park or gazing at the stars from her bedroom window, Swift absorbed the world around her, using it as fuel for her creative fire.

Swift's small town upbringing also instilled in her a profound appreciation for the simplicity of life. She found solace in the rolling hills, the quiet whispers of wind through the trees, and the symphony of crickets on summer nights. These moments of tranquility allowed her to reflect on the passage of time and the ever-changing nature of the world. From the springtime blossoms to the autumn leaves dancing on the breeze, each seasonal shift became a metaphor for growth, loss, and the fleetingness of life.

Beyond the natural beauty, the community itself played a significant role in shaping Swift's character. Wyomissing was not just a place; it was a tight-knit network of friends, neighbors, and mentors. Swift grew up in a supportive environment where her dreams were nurtured and encouraged. Her local community became her biggest cheerleaders, attending her performances, providing guidance, and inspiring her to aim higher.

Through her small town experiences, Swift developed grit and determination. Like any teenager, she faced the struggles of navigating her identity and finding her place in the world. Embracing her love for country music and her dreams of becoming a songwriter set her apart from her peers. Despite the occasional feeling of being an outsider, Swift found solace in her music. She poured her heart and soul into her compositions, using them as a means to connect with others who might have felt the same sense of longing and acceptance.

The small town lifestyle also taught Swift the importance of kindness and community. In Wyomissing, neighbors supported one another, lending a helping hand in times of need and celebrating each other's successes. Swift witnessed firsthand the profound impact simple acts of kindness could have on a person's life and carried these values with her into her career.

Chapter Three

Musical Roots and Influences

T hrough her upbringing and exposure to various genres, Swift developed a deep appreciation for music and honed her skills as a songwriter, culminating in her becoming one of the most influential figures in the industry today.

Influenced by her parents' love for country music, she found herself drawn to the heartfelt storytelling aspect of the genre. Artists such as Shania Twain, Faith Hill, and the Dixie Chicks became significant inspirations as Swift began to navigate her own musical path. She admired their ability to convey raw and honest emotions, capturing the essence of everyday life and relationships within their songs.

However, Swift's musical palette expanded beyond country. Fascinated by the evocative power of different genres, she delved into pop, rock, and even rap music, finding inspiration in the varied melodies and styles. This diverse range of influences would later contribute to the unique blend of genres that would define her sound. From the captivating pop melodies of Britney Spears and NSYNC to the passionate rock anthems of Coldplay and U2, Swift tirelessly studied and absorbed these influences, allowing her to craft a captivating sonic signature that transcended traditional boundaries.

As a teenager, Swift began to explore songwriting with unyielding determination, seeking inspiration from a variety of sources. She found solace in the works of legendary singer-songwriters like Joni Mitchell and Carole King. Their profound impact on her songwriting sensibilities can be heard throughout her early compositions. The introspective lyricism of Mitchell, coupled with King's introspective and confessional approach, resonated deeply with Swift, inspiring her to pen introspective and relatable songs that connected with millions around the world.

Swift's love for storytelling extended beyond music. She often turned to literature and film as additional sources of inspiration, finding creative fuel in the captivating narratives of classic novels and compelling movies. Literary works like Jane Austen's "Pride and Prejudice" and F. Scott Fitzgerald's "The Great Gatsby" captured her imagination with their vivid characters and emotional depth, allowing her to channel their essence into her own songwriting. Alongside these literary influences, movies like Baz Luhrmann's "Romeo + Juliet" and Sofia Coppola's "Lost in Translation" transported her to different worlds, sparking her imagination and prompting her to infuse her songs with captivating imagery and impactful storytelling.

In addition to individual artists and mediums, Swift's collaborations and interactions with fellow musicians have significantly influenced her musical growth. Collaborative projects and tours allowed her to learn from and be inspired by her peers, further expanding her artistic horizons. From iconic collaborations with artists like Ed Sheeran and Kendrick Lamar, where she embraced their unique styles and merged them seamlessly with her own, to memorable duets with country legends such as Tim McGraw and Alison Krauss, Swift's collaborations have been pivotal in her artistic development and have inspired her to constantly challenge herself in her own work.

Chapter Four

Navigating the Nashville Scene

Navigating the Nashville music scene was both a thrilling and challenging experience for the young and ambitious singer-songwriter. Taylor Swift arrived in Nashville with big dreams and a determination to carve out her place in the country music industry.

In the early days, Swift faced numerous rejections, but her unwavering belief in her talent and abilities pushed her to keep going. She often found herself torn between following her heart and adjusting her sound to fit into the traditional country music mold. However, Swift's unique blend of country storytelling and pop sensibilities set her apart from the crowd, and she refused to compromise her artistic vision.

She attended countless open mic nights, showcases, and industry events, honing her skills as a performer and songwriter. Swift quickly became known for her captivating stage presence, leaving audiences mesmerized with her heartfelt performances. Her natural talent for connecting with listeners through her lyrics and her ability to transport them into her world made her a standout artist in Nashville.

As Swift's reputation grew, so did her opportunities. She seized every chance to perform, whether it was on local television shows or by opening for established artists. These experiences helped her to refine her craft and develop her own unique style. Swift's breakout moment came when she secured a publishing deal with Sony/ATV Music Publishing. This partnership provided her with invaluable opportunities to collaborate with seasoned songwriters who helped shape her songwriting skills.

Navigating the Nashville scene also involved building relationships and networking with industry professionals. Swift understood the importance of connecting with those who could open doors for her career. She attended industry events, songwriting seminars, and songwriter rounds, surrounded herself with established songwriters and producers. Through these connections, Swift was able to secure her first record deal with Big Machine Records, a significant step forward in her journey.

However, the journey through the Nashville music scene was not without its challenges. Despite her undeniable talent, Swift faced skepticism from some who doubted her ability to break through. The competitive nature of the industry tested her resilience, making her question whether she would ever reach her dreams. But she stayed true to herself and her craft, continually pushing forward with unwavering determination.

It was during this time that Swift truly found her voice. She embraced her individuality and authenticity, refusing to conform to industry expectations. Her ability to effortlessly blend genres and experiment with sounds allowed her to evolve as an artist and captivate a broader audience. Swift's relatable lyrics and emotional storytelling resonated with listeners far beyond the Nashville music scene, earning her a loyal fanbase that would follow her throughout her career.

Swift's persistence paid off when she released her debut album, "Taylor Swift," which peaked at number five on the Billboard 200 chart. The album's success showcased her ability to craft memorable melodies and poignant lyrics that struck a chord with listeners. Swift's popularity grew rapidly, and she became one of the most promising young artists in Nashville.

Navigating the Nashville scene also meant taking risks and stepping out of her comfort zone. Swift's subsequent albums, such as "Fearless" and "Speak Now," showcased her growth as a songwriter and performer. She fearlessly explored new musical territories, experimenting with different sounds and production techniques. Her evolution as an artist garnered critical acclaim and numerous accolades, solidifying her status as a force to be reckoned with in the music industry.

As her fame skyrocketed, Swift's impact on the music industry extended far beyond Nashville. She became a role model for aspiring artists, demonstrating that hard work, determination, and authenticity can lead to extraordinary success. Swift's philanthropy and activism further solidified her status as a cultural icon, using her platform to advocate for various causes and making a significant impact on social issues.

Chapter Five

Breakthrough in Country Music

Taylor's love for country music blossomed at a young age. Growing up in Pennsylvania, she was drawn to the storytelling aspect of the genre, as well as its ability to evoke genuine emotions. Inspired by artists like Shania Twain and the Dixie Chicks, she studied their music, observing how they crafted their lyrics and melodies to capture the hearts of listeners.

It was this passion for storytelling that led her to Nashville, the heart and soul of country music. With the support of her parents, Swift convinced her family to make the bold move when she was just 14 years old. Nashville offered a unique creative environment, where aspiring artists could connect with like-minded individuals and industry professionals, creating the perfect backdrop for her dreams to flourish.

Upon arriving in Nashville, Swift wasted no time immersing herself in the local music scene. She attended open mic nights, performed at small venues, and actively sought out opportunities to network with fellow musicians and professionals. Her tenacity and determination were unmatched, as she eagerly pursued every chance to showcase her talents and gain valuable experience.

In her pursuit of a breakthrough, Swift caught the attention of Scott Borchetta, a seasoned figure in the music industry who was in the process of launching his own label, Big Machine Records. Recognizing Taylor's potential, Borchetta signed her to the label, offering her the opportunity she had been yearning for - a platform to share her unique voice with the world.

In 2006, Swift released her debut single, "Tim McGraw," a heartfelt ballad that took the country music scene by storm. The song exemplified her ability to infuse vulnerability and relatability into her lyrics, drawing listeners in with its raw emotion. "Tim McGraw" quickly gained traction on country radio, receiving immense support from fans and industry professionals alike.

Swift's self-titled debut album, released that same year, was a testament to her talent as both a songwriter and performer. The album showcased her youthful exuberance, showcased her ability to create infectious melodies, and established her as a rising star in the country music scene. From the catchy "Teardrops on My Guitar" to the introspective "Our Song," the album resonated with listeners of all ages, cementing Swift's status as a force to be reckoned with.

As her popularity soared, Swift made it a priority to connect with her fans on a personal level. She recognized the importance of their support and embarked on a journey to establish a genuine connection with them. Through social media, she shared glimpses of her life and offered a behind-the-scenes look into her creative process. She invited fans to intimate listening parties, where she would share new music and engage in heartfelt conversations. These efforts endeared her to fans, cultivating a loyal and passionate following that would continue to grow with each passing year.

In 2008, Swift released her highly anticipated sophomore album, "Fearless." The album elevated her career to new heights and solidified her as a dominant force in music. "Fearless" showcased her growth as an artist, experimenting with different sounds and incorporating elements of pop, rock, and even a touch of country. The lead single, "Love Story," became a global phenomenon, captivating listeners with its enchanting narrative and timeless appeal. The album went on to win numerous accolades, earning four Grammy Awards, including Album of the Year, making Swift the youngest artist at the time to achieve this honor.

With each subsequent album, Swift continued to break new ground in the country music industry. Her 2010 release, "Speak Now," further showcased her growth as a songwriter, as she took full control of penning all the songs herself. With tracks like "Mine" and "Mean," the album explored themes of personal growth, heartache, and resilience, resonating deeply with her fans. "Speak Now" debuted at number one on the Billboard 200, solidifying her position as a prominent force in the music industry.

As her career progressed, Swift's sound began to evolve even further. Her 2012 album, "Red," signaled a departure from traditional country sounds, embracing a more diverse palette that incorporated elements of pop, rock, and even folk. The album's lead single, "We Are Never Ever Getting Back Together," marked the beginning of her crossover into the pop world, while tracks like "I Knew You Were Trouble" showcased her willingness to experiment with new sounds and push the boundaries of her artistry. "Red" debuted at number one on the Billboard 200, selling a staggering 1.2 million copies in its first week.

Taylor Swift's breakthrough in the country music industry not only marked her rise to stardom but also left an indelible impact on the genre itself. Her success opened doors for other young female artists, inspiring a new generation of songwriters to share their stories authentically and unapologetically. As she pushed the boundaries of country music, Swift challenged traditional notions, paving the way for a more diverse and inclusive landscape within the genre.

Chapter Six

From Fearless to Red: Exploring Swift's Evolution

This era marked a significant shift in Swift's career as she transitioned from a country darling to a pop icon.

"Fearless," released in 2008, propelled Taylor Swift to new heights of fame and success. The album not only showcased her incredible talent as a singer-songwriter but also broke records and earned her numerous accolades. Its catchy melodies and relatable lyrics immediately resonated with fans worldwide. Swift's ability to encapsulate the emotions and experiences of an entire generation made her appeal universal. Tracks like "Love Story," "You Belong with Me," and "Fifteen" became anthems for young people navigating love and heartbreak. Swift's empathetic and vulnerable nature captivated listeners, earning her critical acclaim and commercial success.

However, Swift's evolution didn't stop there. With the release of "Speak Now" in 2010, she demonstrated her growth as a songwriter and musician. Taking full creative control, Swift wrote every song on the album, showcasing her maturity and artistic vision. "Speak Now" allowed Swift to further establish herself as a force to be reckoned with in the music industry. Hits like "Mine," "Back to December," and "Mean" showcased her ability to capture both personal experiences and universal emotions. Swift's ability to craft emotionally charged narratives with witty wordplay and heartfelt melodies stood out, earning her respect and admiration from fans and critics alike.

The true turning point in Swift's career, however, came with the release of "Red" in 2012. This album marked a significant departure from her previous work, showcasing her artistic growth and inclination towards stepping outside genre boundaries. Motivated by a desire to explore new musical horizons, Swift embraced a more pop-infused sound, which surprised many of her long-time country music followers. Although some were initially skeptical about the change, "Red" was met with resounding success, ultimately exceeding expectations. Swift's collaboration with Max Martin and Shellback, renowned pop hitmakers, brought a newfound energy and polished production to her music. Tracks like "We Are Never Ever Getting Back Together," "I Knew You Were Trouble," and "22" showcased her evolution as an artist.

The lyrical content of "Red" explored a broader range of emotions, capturing the highs and lows of love and heartbreak with unfiltered honesty. Swift's songwriting reached new depths, resonating with listeners on a personal level. Each track on the album painted a different shade of Swift's experiences, allowing fans to see her growth and maturity. From the heart-wrenching ballads like "All Too Well" to the infectious pop anthems like "22," Swift demonstrated her ability to express her emotions in a way that was relatable to millions of people around the world.

"Red" also showcased Swift's versatility as a musician. The album incorporated elements of various genres, including pop, rock, folk, and even dubstep. By blending these diverse sounds seamlessly, Swift proved her ability to experiment with different styles while maintaining her unique voice and artistic identity. This willingness to explore new territory ultimately paid off, as "Red" became one of the best-selling albums of the year and further solidified Swift's status as a dominant force in the music industry.

However, Swift's evolution during this period wasn't limited to her music. She also underwent a significant transformation in her public image. Shedding her country girl image, Swift embraced a more mature and sophisticated look. Her fashion choices became a topic of discussion, and Swift's influence on the fashion industry began to gain recognition. From her signature red lip to her elegant red-carpet appearances, Swift became a style icon, making waves in the fashion world.

Beyond her music and fashion, Swift's impact extended into various philanthropic endeavors. She used her platform to advocate for causes close to her heart, such as education, disaster relief, and music education. Swift's generosity and dedication to giving back created a powerful connection with her fans, further solidifying her status as a role model.

Chapter Seven

Transition to Pop: 1989 and Beyond

This pivotal moment marked a significant turning point in her career and solidified her status as a global pop sensation.

Taylor Swift's decision to venture into pop music was fueled by a variety of factors. As an artist committed to personal growth and reinvention, she sought to explore new sonic territories, experiment with different musical styles, and challenge herself creatively. Additionally, the changing landscape of the music industry played a significant role in her transition. With the rise of digital platforms and the decline of traditional album sales, Swift recognized the need to evolve and appeal to a broader audience.

The making of "1989" was a defining period for Swift. Fueled by the desire to reinvent herself and break free from the confines of the country music genre, she embarked on an intense period of soul-searching and self-discovery. Drawing inspiration from the vibrant music scene of New York City, Swift repeatedly immersed herself in its infectious energy, attending concerts, collaborating with fellow artists, and soaking up the diverse sounds that surrounded her.

Collaborating with renowned pop producers like Max Martin and Shellback, Swift embraced a meticulously crafted pop sound characterized by infectious hooks, synth-driven melodies, and pulsating beats. This infusion of contemporary pop elements transformed her music into an undeniable force on mainstream radio. The sonic evolution was evident in the album's lead single, "Shake It Off," which marked a departure from her signature country sound. The lively and catchy track became an instant anthem of self-acceptance and resilience, resonating with audiences worldwide.

However, the transition to pop wasn't without its challenges. Swift faced criticisms and skepticism from some fans and industry insiders who doubted her ability to successfully navigate a new genre. Accused of abandoning her country roots, she faced a backlash that questioned her authenticity. However, Swift's unwavering conviction in her artistic choices enabled her to rise above the noise and chart her own course.

Beyond the musical shift, Swift's transition to pop represented a significant evolution in her public image and persona. She shed her "girl-next-door" image and embraced a more glamorous and edgy aesthetic. This transformation was evident in her music videos, stage performances, and overall persona, allowing her to connect with a wider audience and establish herself as a force to be reckoned with in the pop landscape.

"1989" showcased Swift's growth as a songwriter. She honed her ability to craft relatable and emotionally charged stories, capturing the complexities of love, heartbreak, and self-discovery. Tracks like "Style," "Blank Space," and "Bad Blood" showcased her ability to write catchy hooks without sacrificing substance, resonating with millions of listeners across the globe. The album's introspective and vulnerable tracks, such as "Wildest Dreams" and "Out of the Woods," demonstrated Swift's ability to delve into deeper emotional territory while maintaining broad commercial appeal.

The success of "1989" catapulted Swift into new realms of stardom and solidified her status as one of the biggest pop superstars of the decade. The album received critical acclaim and dominated the charts, staying at number one in the Billboard 200 chart for multiple weeks. It went on to win numerous awards, including multiple Grammy Awards, with the prestigious Album of the Year being one of its crowning achievements.

Chapter Eight

Love, Heartbreak, and the Art of Songwriting

Love and heartbreak are recurring themes in her songwriting, offering listeners a glimpse into her most intimate experiences and emotions.

Throughout her discography, Swift fearlessly explores the complexities of love, capturing both the euphoria of new romance and the pain of shattered relationships. Her ability to articulate the intricacies of human connection and vulnerability has resonated with millions, making her one of the most relatable artists of our time.

From the innocence and naivety of her early hits such as "Love Story" and "You Belong with Me" to the introspection and maturity found in later tracks like "Blank Space" and "Delicate," Swift's journey through love and heartbreak is a rollercoaster that listeners can't help but ride alongside her.

What sets Swift apart as a songwriter is her unmatched ability to extract beauty from heartache. Her music not only encompasses the emotional whirlwind that love and heartbreak bring, but also addresses the lessons learned and personal growth that arises from these experiences. Swift embraces the bruises left by love and examines them from all angles, weaving together lyrics that resonate deeply with anyone who has ever loved and lost.

In each song, Swift becomes an emotional architect, constructing narratives filled with vivid imagery and relatable metaphors. She invites her audience into her heart and mind, revealing the intricate details of her relationships, the moments of pure joy and the heart-wrenching fragments of loss. There is an authenticity to her storytelling, leaving no emotion unexplored, no sentiment unexpressed.

Whether it's the raw vulnerability of "All Too Well," a masterpiece that chronicles the demise of a once passionate relationship, or the empowering resilience of "Shake It Off," an anthem that celebrates shaking off heartbreak and embracing self-love, Swift's authentic storytelling has touched the hearts of millions.

Swift's lyrical skill doesn't stop at recounting her own experiences. She has an uncanny ability to tap into the collective human experience of love and heartbreak. Her songs become mirrors through which listeners see their own reflections, finding solace in the fact that someone else understands their deepest fears, hopes, and desires.

Chapter Nine

Swift's Unparalleled Connection with Fans

One of the defining characteristics of Taylor Swift's career has been her unparalleled connection with her fans. From the very beginning, Swift recognized the importance of building a close relationship with her supporters and has gone above and beyond to create a unique bond that sets her apart in the music industry.

Swift's connection with her fans started early in her career when she would personally respond to messages and comments on social media platforms like MySpace and Facebook. It was through these interactions that she learned about her fans' dreams, struggles, and experiences. Swift understood that her success was rooted in the people who listened to her music, and she wanted to express her gratitude in a genuine and personal way.

As her fanbase grew exponentially with each album release, Swift found creative ways to engage with her fans on a larger scale. She would send personalized gifts and handwritten letters to fans, showing them that she saw and valued their support. These gestures were not just acts of appreciation but also opportunities for Swift to connect with her fans on an emotional level.

In 2014, Swift took her connection with fans to new heights with the "Swiftmas" campaign. She scoured the internet, searching for her fans and learning about their personal stories. Swift dedicated countless hours to understanding their lives and interests, allowing her to curate the perfect gifts for each individual. From surprise packages filled with personal mementos to concert tickets and exclusive merchandise, the "Swiftmas" campaign was a testament to Swift's unwavering commitment to her fans.

But Swift's dedication to her fans goes beyond material gifts. She genuinely cares about their well-being and takes the time to interact with them in meaningful ways. Whether it's engaging with fans' social media posts, surprising them with impromptu visits or phone calls, or taking photos with them at her concerts, Swift constantly seeks opportunities for connection. She understands the power of a simple conversation or a shared moment and the impact it can have on someone's life.

Furthermore, Swift constantly looks for ways to involve her fans in her creative process. She has been known to hold secret listening sessions for her albums, inviting a select group of fans to get an exclusive first listen before the official release. This intimate experience not only allows her fans to feel connected to her music but also makes them feel like active participants in her artistic journey. Swift values their opinions and insights, often seeking their feedback and incorporating their stories into her songwriting.

Swift takes pride in creating a community where her fans can support each other. She encourages her fans to connect with one another, fostering an environment of friendship and kindness. On social media, Swift often promotes fan accounts and actively engages in discussions, amplifying their voices and showing appreciation for their love and dedication. This sense of unity and camaraderie within the fanbase has contributed to the strong and lasting connection they share with Swift.

Swift's commitment to her fans extends beyond the realm of music. She uses her platform to empower and uplift her fanbase. She has supported causes close to her fans' hearts, advocated for positive change, and used her influence to speak out against injustice. Whether it's donating to charities, raising awareness about important issues, or organizing charitable events, Swift's actions reflect the depth of her connection with her fans. Through these acts of generosity and inclusivity, she fosters a supportive community that seeks to make a difference in the world.

In turn, Swift's fans have become an integral part of her success. They have played a crucial role in promoting her music, advocating for her during challenging times, and creating a supportive environment at her concerts and online platforms. Swift recognizes the significance of her fans in her career and often acknowledges their invaluable support in acceptance speeches and social media posts. She sees herself as a partner in their lives, cherishing their stories, and understanding the impact she has on their emotions and experiences.

Chapter Ten

Taking a Stand: Advocacy and Empowerment

In addition to being a talented musician and songwriter, Taylor Swift has also been a powerful advocate for various causes and a champion of empowerment. Throughout her career, she has used her platform to raise awareness and spark conversations about important social and political issues, leaving an indelible mark on the world of activism.

One of the causes that Swift has been vocal about is feminism. She has consistently advocated for women's rights and equality, using her lyrics and public statements to address gender inequality and encourage women to speak up and stand tall. Swift recognizes that feminism is not about superiority or diminishing men but about fostering a society where individuals are not limited or judged based on their gender. Her song "The Man" is a prime example of this, as she tackles gender double standards and the systematic biases that women face in society. By boldly challenging societal norms and expectations, she pushes boundaries and inspires women around the globe to assert their worth and demand equal treatment.

Beyond her feminist activism, Swift has also been a prominent voice in the fight against sexual assault. In 2017, she took former radio DJ David Mueller to court for groping her during a photo op. Despite the public scrutiny and potential backlash, Swift stood her ground and spoke out against sexual harassment, sending a resounding message that abuse and assault will not be tolerated. While the trial focused on her own experience, she recognized the larger importance of using her platform to shed light on the pervasive issue of sexual assault. Her courage and unwavering determination sent shockwaves through society, fueling the ongoing conversation about consent and the importance of believing survivors. Swift's personal journey from victim to survivor has been an inspiration to many, and her unwavering commitment to justice and her refusal to be silenced have inspired countless survivors to find their own voice and seek the justice they deserve.

Education is another cause close to Swift's heart. She recognizes the transformative power of a quality education and believes that every child should have access to it. Swift has donated generously to various schools and educational programs, emphasizing the importance of breaking down barriers and ensuring equal opportunities for all. Moreover, she actively supports organizations that promote literacy, particularly among underprivileged children, understanding that education is the key to unlocking a brighter future for individuals and communities alike. Swift's dedication to education is exemplified through the establishment of the Taylor Swift Education Center at the Country Music Hall of Fame and Museum, a space that inspires young people to explore and engage with music and its associated educational opportunities, fostering creativity and growth.

In recent years, Swift has become an influential advocate for LGBTQ+ rights. She has openly embraced and supported the community, using her platform to champion acceptance and equality. Whether it's through her music videos, public speeches, or social media posts, Swift sends a clear message of support and solidarity to the LGBTQ+ community, effectively using her influence to promote positive change. She has actively raised awareness about the issues faced by LGBTQ+ individuals, from discrimination and inequality to the struggle for acceptance and self-discovery. Swift's unwavering allyship has not only fostered a more inclusive and accepting society but has also provided comfort and hope to countless LGBTQ+ individuals who have felt marginalized or alone. Her participation in events such as the Stonewall Inn's 50th anniversary celebration and her donation to LGBTQ+ organizations like GLAAD further highlight her commitment to the cause.

One of the most remarkable aspects of Swift's advocacy work is her connection with her fans, affectionately known as the Swifties. She has cultivated a strong and dedicated following, fostering a sense of belonging and empowerment among her fans. Swift often interacts with her fans on social media, listening to their stories, offering support, and amplifying their voices. This active engagement creates a dialogue and a community built on mutual respect and understanding. Swift recognizes the power of her platform and actively uses it to uplift her fans, reminding them to embrace their uniqueness, stand up for what they believe in, and never underestimate their ability to effect change.

The collective energy and activism of the Swifties serve as a testament to the impact she has had on her fans' lives, and their shared values further reinforce the importance of advocacy and empowerment. Swift has also utilized her platform to encourage her fans to get involved in various initiatives and organizations that align with her causes. Through social media campaigns and public partnerships, she has inspired her fans to take action, whether it's volunteering, donating, or simply spreading awareness.

Chapter Eleven

The Media's Love-Hate Relationship

In the highly scrutinized world of fame, Taylor Swift has had her fair share of love and hate from the media. From the beginning of her career, she captured the attention of tabloids and paparazzi, eager to uncover every detail of her personal life. As a young woman navigating the complexities of fame, Swift became a target for gossip and relentless speculation.

In the early years, the media often portrayed Swift as the innocent girl-next-door with a string of high-profile romances. Her relationships were dissected by the press, with headlines splashed across magazines and websites. It seemed that her personal life became a favorite topic for rumor mills, creating a narrative that overshadowed her musical achievements.

But Swift refused to be defined solely by her relationships. She used her music as a way to reclaim her narrative, writing candidly about her experiences and emotions. Through heartfelt lyrics and infectious melodies, Swift connected with millions of fans who related to her vulnerability and resilience.

As her career progressed, Swift's image began to shift. With each album release, she experimented with different musical styles and personas, evolving into a stronger, more empowered artist. However, this evolution was not always met favorably by the media.

Critics accused her of "playing the victim" and called into question her authenticity. Swift faced backlash for her bold statements and unapologetic approach to her artistry. The media seemed to both love and loathe her at the same time, torn between recognizing her talent and scrutinizing her every move.

Swift's relationship with the media reached a turning point with the infamous "Kanye incident" at the 2009 MTV Video Music Awards. This incident, where Kanye West infamously interrupted her acceptance speech, sparked a media frenzy and led to a significant shift in public perception. Swift was seen as a victim, and the media couldn't get enough of the story.

In the years that followed, Swift used her platform to speak out against the pressures and injustices of the entertainment industry. She called out unfair treatment, fought for artists' rights, and used her voice to address social issues. While some praised her for using her fame for good, others criticized her for being too outspoken or accused her of seeking attention.

The media's love-hate relationship with Swift became increasingly complex as she redefined her image with the release of her album, "1989." Departing from her country roots, she embraced a pop sound that appealed to a wider audience. The media marveled at her ability to reinvent herself, but also questioned her authenticity in this new realm.

The scrutiny intensified as Swift's love life continued to be a topic of interest. Her high-profile relationships with celebrities such as Harry Styles and Tom Hiddleston garnered significant media attention. Some praised her for fearlessly pursuing love, while others criticized her for what they perceived as a calculated PR strategy.

Despite the criticisms, Swift's talent and work ethic were undeniable. Her songwriting prowess earned her numerous accolades, including multiple Grammy Awards. Each new album release was eagerly anticipated by fans and the media alike, as they waited to see what personal and artistic revelations she would share.

Swift's reputation took another hit during a highly publicized feud with fellow artist Kanye West and his wife, Kim Kardashian. It all began with West's controversial song lyrics, which Swift claimed painted her in a negative light. The ensuing media frenzy highlighted a narrative of Swift as an unreliable narrator, and she faced a wave of criticism and online harassment.

Facing the intensified scrutiny, Swift retreated from the public eye, taking a hiatus from music. During this period, she focused on introspection, personal growth, and self-reflection. Swift used her time away to recalibrate her relationship with the media and how she want-ed to be perceived.

When she returned with her album "Reputation," Swift surprised everyone with a new level of self-assuredness and defiance. She embraced her flaws and past controversies, channeling them into a body of work that further cemented her status as a resilient artist. While the media initially questioned her intentions, many eventually acknowledged the renewed authenticity and vulnerability in her music.

In recent years, Swift has continued to evolve and grow as an artist. Her willingness to experiment with different genres and tackle complex subjects in her songwriting has solidified her status as a respected figure in the music industry. The media's love-hate relationship with Swift has mellowed, as her constant evolution and undeniable talent have earned her a place as one of the most influential artists of her generation.

Throughout it all, Swift's ability to connect with her fans remained unwavering. She understood the power of her influence and used it to create a community that supported and uplifted one another. In the face of media backlash, her fans became a source of strength and refuge.

The media's love-hate relationship with Taylor Swift is a testament to her enduring impact on popular culture. Despite the challenges and controversies, she has remained true to herself and continued to reinvent her sound and image. Swift's ability to navigate the often treacherous waters of fame with grace and resilience sets her apart as not only a talented artist but also a symbol of empowerment for her fans around the world.

As Swift continues to evolve in her music and her public persona, the media's perception of her has slowly shifted. They have come to appreciate her authenticity and vulnerability, recognizing the growth in her artistry. The love-hate relationship that once plagued their coverage of her has transformed into a respect for her talent and enduring influence.

Swift's ability to take control of her narrative through her music has been a driving force in reshaping the media's portrayal of her. With each album release, she offers a glimpse into her personal experiences, showcasing her growth, resilience, and self-reflection. This transparency has allowed her fans to connect with her on a profound level, and it has also given the media a deeper understanding of the artist beyond the headlines.

The media's love-hate relationship with Swift is not unique to her alone. In the world of celebrity, this dynamic often emerges when artists rise to superstardom. The media builds them up, only to tear them down, scrutinizing their every move and exploiting their personal lives for profit. Swift has managed to navigate this volatile landscape with grace, driven by her unwavering dedication to her craft and her sincere connection with her fans.

Chapter Twelve

Swift's Impact on Fashion and Culture

T aylor isn't just known for her music, but also for her impeccable sense of fashion and her profound influence on popular culture. Over the years, Swift has become a fashion icon, constantly reinventing her style and setting trends that are eagerly followed by fans and fashion enthusiasts alike.

From her early country music days to her transition into pop, Swift's fashion choices have evolved along with her music, capturing the essence of each era she embarks on. In the beginning, she often embraced a more wholesome and girl-next-door aesthetic, with flowing sundresses, cowboy boots, and her signature curly hair. This look resonated perfectly with her country music roots, connecting profoundly with her young and wide-eyed fan base at the time.

As Swift's music expanded beyond the country genre, her fashion sense also underwent a transformative journey. She started experimenting with edgier looks, incorporating more bold colors, sleek silhouettes, and fashion-forward designs. Swift's red carpet appearances became highly anticipated events, where she would make statements with her outfits that would ignite conversations and inspire fashion trends.

One of Swift's most memorable fashion moments came in 2014 when she released her highly successful album "1989". This marked a significant turning point in her career, causing her to fully embrace the pop music scene. During this time, she embraced a more modern and sophisticated style, often seen in crop tops, high-waisted skirts, and bold red lipstick. This era solidified her reputation as a fashion risk-taker, confidently exploring her artistry and setting new standards for the industry.

Swift's influence on fashion extends beyond her own wardrobe choices. She has collaborated with several fashion brands, showcasing her versatility and appealing to a wider audience. Her partnerships with brands such as Keds, Diet Coke, and most notably, her collaboration with designer Stella McCartney, have allowed Swift to extend her influence and create fashion lines that authentically reflect her personal style. Emphasizing the importance of inclusivity, her collaborations promoted diverse representations of beauty within the fashion industry.

Furthermore, Swift has been praised for her body-positive message and her commitment to promoting inclusivity and diversity in the fashion industry. She has spoken out about the unrealistic beauty standards that pervade the industry and has actively supported designers and brands that embrace diversity and celebrate different body types and backgrounds. Swift's acceptance and celebration of her own body has resonated with fans and has created a significant space for more diverse representations of beauty in the fashion world.

Chapter Thirteen

From Stage to Screen: Swift's Venture into Acting

While primarily known for her chart-topping music and heartfelt songwriting, Swift has also made notable appearances on the big and small screens, showcasing her versatility as an entertainer and deepening her connection with fans.

Swift's acting debut came in 2009 with a memorable role in the ensemble romantic comedy film "Valentine's Day." Directed by the late Garry Marshall, the film boasted a star-studded cast including Julia Roberts, Ashton Kutcher, and Jessica Alba. With her role as Felicia Miller, a high school student experiencing a bittersweet first love, Swift revealed her ability to bring depth and emotion to her on-screen characters. While the film received mixed reviews from critics, Swift's performance garnered positive attention, demonstrating her natural aptitude for acting.

With her foot firmly planted in the acting world, Swift took on her most prominent role to date in 2010 as Bombalurina in the highly anticipated musical adaptation of Andrew Lloyd Webber's iconic stage production, "Cats." Directed by the visionary Tom Hooper, the film aimed to bring the beloved musical to a wider audience. Despite receiving mixed reviews from critics, with some praising its visual spectacle and others critiquing its execution, Swift's performance stood out. As Bombalurina, a flirtatious and confident cat, Swift showcased her vocal prowess and thrilled audiences with her captivating presence. Her dedication to the role, overcoming the challenges faced during the film's production, showcased her commitment as a performer and her ability to shine in different mediums.

While her film roles have garnered significant attention, Swift has also made notable guest appearances on television shows and series, further diversifying her acting portfolio. In 2009, she made a memorable cameo as herself on an episode of the popular crime procedural "CSI: Crime Scene Investigation." In the episode titled "Turn, Turn, Turn," Swift played the character of Haley Jones, a rebellious teenager with a talent for music who finds herself entangled in a murder investigation. This guest appearance marked Swift's television acting debut and showcased her ability to captivate audiences in different mediums.

Another noteworthy television appearance came in 2013 when Swift guest-starred on the hit sitcom "New Girl." In the episode titled "Elaine's Big Day," she played Elaine, a wedding guest who catches the attention of the main character, Jess, portrayed by Zooey Deschanel. Swift's comedic timing and charisma shone through in this role, earning her praise for her acting skills and further highlighting her versatility as a performer. Her portrayal of Elaine showcased her ability to seamlessly blend into an established ensemble cast and deliver a memorable performance.

Swift's venture into acting has allowed her to expand her creative horizons and explore different facets of storytelling. While her primary focus remains on her music career, her acting endeavors have added depth to her artistic repertoire, captivating audiences in new ways. Through her roles on both the big and small screens, she has demonstrated versatility, depth, and a willingness to embrace new challenges, cementing her status as a multi-talented artist.

Chapter Fourteen

Philanthropy and Humanitarian Work

T hroughout her career, she has consistently used her platform to make a difference in the world through philanthropy and humanitarian work. Swift's commitment to various causes demonstrates her genuine desire to create positive change, inspiring others to join her in making a lasting impact.

One of the causes closest to Swift's heart is education. In 2009, she donated $250,000 to her own high school, Hendersonville High, to fund improvements to the school's auditorium. This act of generosity exemplified her belief in the transformative power of education and set a precedent for her future philanthropic endeavors.

Recognizing the importance of music education, Swift donated $75,000 to the Nashville Symphony in 2010, specifically directing the funds towards music education programs. She believes that by providing young individuals with access to music education, they can develop invaluable skills and ignite their passion for the arts. This support not only benefits individual students but also contributes to the enrichment of communities as a whole.

In 2013, Swift took her commitment to education one step further. She launched the Taylor Swift Education Center at the Country Music Hall of Fame and Museum, an innovative facility designed to provide educational resources, interactive exhibits, and hands-on experiences for students of all ages. This center stands as a testament to Swift's dedication to fostering creativity and nurturing talent, regardless of one's background or circumstances. By creating a space that combines music, history, and education, Swift has empowered countless individuals to pursue their dreams and embrace lifelong learning.

Beyond education, Swift has demonstrated a deep commitment to humanitarian efforts. As a long-standing supporter of the Red Cross, she has made substantial donations to aid disaster relief efforts worldwide. Her contributions have helped provide essential resources and support to communities affected by natural disasters, facilitating the process of recovery and rebuilding.

Furthermore, Swift has used her platform to raise awareness and funds for crucial causes. In 2012, she partnered with Stand Up to Cancer, a non-profit organization dedicated to accelerating cancer research, and performed a heartfelt tribute song, "Ronan," dedicated to a young boy who had lost his battle with cancer. The proceeds from this emotional song were donated to support groundbreaking cancer research and create hope for individuals and families affected by this devastating disease. Through her art, Swift serves as a powerful advocate for those who face adversity and amplifies their voices.

In addition to her charitable contributions, Swift has become an advocate for women's rights and safety. In 2017, she stood up against sexual assault and successfully sued a radio host for a symbolic $1 after he groped her during a photo op. Her decision to take legal action sent a powerful message to survivors of assault, highlighting the importance of speaking out and seeking justice. Swift's bold stance inspired others to come forward, sparking a global conversation about consent and the need for a societal shift in attitudes towards women's bodily autonomy.

Chapter Fifteen

The Reputation Era: Trials and Triumphs

The Reputation era began in 2017 with the release of Swift's sixth studio album, aptly titled "Reputation." The album marked a significant departure from her previous sound, embracing a darker and more experimental tone. It was a deliberate move to address the controversies and media scrutiny she had faced in the past.

Swift, known for her relatability and heartfelt storytelling, took a daring step by immersing herself in a more mysterious and enigmatic persona. The first taste of this new chapter came with the release of the lead single, "Look What You Made Me Do." The song incorporated a sample from Right Said Fred's "I'm Too Sexy" and showcased Swift's biting lyrics, symbolizing her willingness to take control of her narrative.

Yet, the anticipation surrounding the release of "Reputation" was met with mixed reactions. Critics questioned her artistic direction, suggesting that she had abandoned her roots, while others praised her audacity and growth. It was clear that Swift was embarking on a uncharted path, determined to challenge both herself and her audience.

The media scrutiny surrounding Swift was at an all-time high during the Reputation era. Her personal life and relationships were dissected endlessly in tabloids and gossip columns. Swift found herself at the center of numerous controversies, often being branded as a manipulative and calculating figure. The public narratives surrounding her became tangled, creating a cloud of judgment that hung over her every move.

However, beneath the surface of these controversies, Swift's determination to rise above it all was unwavering. She refused to let herself be defined by the media's portrayal of her. Instead, she used her music and platform to face her detractors head-on. In tracks like "Delicate," she delved deep into her vulnerabilities, acknowledging the impact of the negativity she faced and the weight it carried on her psyche.

The Reputation era was not just about reclaiming her narrative, but also about cultivating a sense of empowerment within herself and her fans. Swift empowered her listeners to embrace their own identities and navigate the complexities of personal growth. The album's introspective tracks like "Getaway Car" and "Call It What You Want" painted a picture of self-reflection and resilience, proving that Swift had indeed grown from her experiences.

Amidst the trials, the Reputation Stadium Tour emerged as a shining beacon of triumph. Launched in 2018, it showcased Swift's charisma and talent on a grand scale. The tour was not merely a concert; it was a visual spectacle that left audiences in awe. Swift's performances featured larger-than-life production, intricate stage designs, and choreographed routines that elevated the live experience to a whole new level. At each show, she commanded the massive stadiums with her captivating presence, leaving an indelible mark on fans' hearts.

Beyond her tour, Swift's willingness to engage with her fans on personal levels set her apart as a genuine and caring artist. She surprised them by hosting listening parties at her own home, personally delivering gifts to dedicated fans, and interacting with them on social media. These gestures solidified the bond between Swift and her fans, creating a deeply connected community who stood by her side throughout the era.

Chapter Sixteen

Lover: A Celebration of Love and Self-Discovery

With its vibrant pastel aesthetics and heartfelt lyricism, "Lover" resonated powerfully with fans around the world, becoming an anthem of empowerment and emotional exploration. Swift invited listeners into her most intimate thoughts and experiences, going beyond the conventional idea of love and delving into the depths of human connection.

The album's title track, "Lover," sets the tone for the entire record. It captures the essence of a deep and enduring love that transcends time and circumstance, a sentiment that Swift masterfully weaves throughout the album. The song celebrates the beauty of a committed relationship and the security that comes from finding a true partner, painting a vivid picture of lovers finding solace and refuge within each other. By expressing unwavering love and loyalty, Swift encourages listeners to embrace the vulnerability and strength that love brings.

Yet, "Lover" is not limited to romantic love alone. Swift courageously expands her exploration of love to include the love we have for ourselves and the journey of self-discovery. In the track "The Archer," she reflects on her own insecurities and struggles with self-doubt, acknowledging that true growth and self-acceptance come from confronting our inner demons. The song becomes an anthem of self-discovery, urging listeners to dig deep within themselves, face their fears, and embark on a transformative journey of self-acceptance. Swift's vulnerability and introspection create a safe space for fans to acknowledge their own flaws and begin their own path towards self-love and personal growth.

Additionally, "Lover" touches upon the complexities of societal pressures, gender norms, and the need for inclusivity. In "You Need to Calm Down," Swift takes a powerful stand against discrimination and advocates for the LGBTQ+ community. Through the use of catchy melodies and thought-provoking lyrics, she urges listeners to build a more accepting and loving world, emphasizing the importance of unity and understanding. Swift demonstrates her growth as an artist and as an individual, using her platform to push for positive change and challenge societal norms.

The album's production and songwriting showcase a creative evolution that is both refreshing and authentic. Swift fearlessly experiments with new sounds and genres while staying true to her distinctive songwriting style, resulting in tracks like the vibrant and whimsical "London Boy" or the heartfelt and nostalgic "Cornelia Street." These songs, among others, exude a magical aura, conjuring up vivid imagery and evoking a range of emotions in listeners. The emotional depth and introspection present in the lyrics allow listeners to become fully immersed in Swift's world and, simultaneously, reflect on their own experiences with love and self-discovery.

One of the standout tracks, "The Man," delivers a powerful message about gender inequality and the double standards women face in society. Swift's introspective and incisive lyrics spotlight the different treatment she would receive if she were a man, challenging societal norms and shedding light on the inherent biases that still prevail. By tackling this subject matter head-on, Swift uses her platform to advocate for gender equality and encourages her fans to do the same. The message resonates deeply, further solidifying "Lover" as an album that is not just about personal narratives but also as a catalyst for social change.

"Lover" is not just an album; it is a testament to Swift's growth as an artist and as an individual. It showcases her ability to evolve both musically and personally, exploring new sounds while remaining true to her distinctive songwriting style. Through the celebration of love and self-discovery, Swift invites us to confront our own emotions, reflect on our relationships, and find solace in the universal experiences of the human heart. "Lover" is a testament to the transformative power of love and the courage it takes to embrace our truest selves, ultimately guiding us towards a journey of self-acceptance and personal growth.

Folklore and Evermore: Swift's Pandemic Creative Journey

"Folklore," released on July 24, 2020, marked a departure from Swift's previous pop-infused sound. This indie folk album was a revelation, showcasing her versatility and maturity as a songwriter. With introspective and poetic lyrics, each song became a vivid story woven seamlessly into the fabric of the album. Collaborating with Aaron Dessner of The National and other talented musicians remotely, Swift managed to create a cohesive and hauntingly beautiful record.

The inception of "Folklore" came from Swift's introspective journey during the pandemic, reflecting on her own thoughts and emotions, as well as incorporating fictional tales and characters. Fueled by her fascination with storytelling in its various forms, she delved deep into the realms of poetry, literature, and even cinema to shape the narrative arc of the album. Drawing inspiration from great works like "Wuthering Heights" by Emily Brontë and movies like "The Last Great American Dynasty," Swift crafted a rich tapestry of interconnected tales.

The album's lead single, "Cardigan," introduced listeners to a magical world filled with nostalgia and longing. It set the tone for what became a conceptual masterpiece, interweaving narratives about love, loss, and personal growth. Each subsequent track held its own distinct identity, allowing listeners to step into different stories and explore the complex emotions they contained.

The creative process for "Folklore" was uniquely crafted with virtual collaborations and remote recording sessions. Swift and her collaborators employed inventive methods to create an intimate atmosphere despite being physically separated. Through video calls, voice memos, and digital file-sharing, they brought their individual contributions to life and merged them into an extraordinary sonic tapestry. The album's production exuded a sense of rawness and authenticity, enhancing the storytelling experience.

Only five months later, on December 11, 2020, Swift surprised the world yet again with "Evermore." Considered a companion album to "Folklore," "Evermore" continued to explore introspection and storytelling with a touch of whimsy. Swift effortlessly shifted between genres, seamlessly blending folk, alternative, and pop elements.

"Evermore" was built upon the foundation laid by "Folklore," diving deeper into the world established in its predecessor. Swift expanded her creative vision, exploring untrodden paths to convey a multitude of emotions. The album's standout track, "Willow," showcased Swift's ability to craft ethereal melodies with pointed lyrics, creating a mesmerizing and cinematic experience for her listeners.

The release of "Evermore" once again proved Swift's determination to push creative boundaries and challenge herself as an artist. Collaborating with long-time friend and musician Justin Vernon, of Bon Iver, Swift struck a delicate balance between melancholic storytelling and uplifting melodies. Each song on the album felt like a chapter in an ongoing saga, further unraveling the intricate layers of Swift's imagination and allowing listeners to witness the evolution of her storytelling prowess.

Both albums were met with overwhelming praise from fans and critics alike. Swift's decision to embrace a more indie folk-oriented sound showcased her artistic evolution and her willingness to embrace vulnerability and introspection. The depth of her storytelling and the emotional resonance of her lyrics demonstrated a level of maturity and growth in her craft.

From the intricate instrumentation to the evocative lyrics, "Folklore" and "Evermore" captured the essence of a world in turmoil, offering solace and escapism to listeners navigating their own personal struggles. Swift masterfully translated her own experiences into universal tales that spoke to the human condition, allowing her listeners to find solace and understanding amidst uncertain times.

Chapter Eighteen

Legacy and Influence: Taylor Swift's Enduring Impact

Taylor's profound influence on the music industry and popular culture transcends time and continues to evolve. Her enduring impact is rooted in the unique way she has connected with her audience, the fearless exploration of her sound, and her powerful advocacy for pivotal social issues.

One of the defining aspects of Taylor Swift's impact is her remarkable ability to forge deep emotional connections with her listeners. From the very beginning of her career, she displayed an uncanny ability to communicate the raw and relatable emotions experienced by young people navigating love, heartbreak, and self-discovery. Through her deeply introspective songwriting, she has become a voice for her fans, expressing their innermost thoughts and feelings. Swift's vulnerability and authenticity have created an unbreakable bond between artist and listener, making her music an integral part of fans' lives.

Through the years, Taylor Swift's evolution as an artist has been nothing short of extraordinary. From her early days as a country-pop crossover sensation to her bold transition into pure pop music, she has fearlessly challenged expectations and defied genre conventions. Swift's willingness to experiment and push boundaries has propelled her sound to new heights, leading to innovative collaborations and chart-topping hits. Drawing inspiration from an eclectic mix of musical genres, she has seamlessly fused elements of pop, rock, electronic, and even alternative music into her repertoire, captivating a wider range of listeners.

Beyond her musical prowess, Taylor Swift's impactful philanthropic efforts and activism have solidified her as a force for positive change. She has utilized her platform to advocate for and raise awareness about numerous causes, including education, disaster relief, and fighting for equal rights. Swift's philanthropic endeavors extend far beyond monetary donations, as she has also engaged in meaningful dialogue with fans and used her influence to amplify marginalized voices. By actively supporting organizations such as the Red Cross, UNICEF, and various LGBTQ+ charities, she has inspired her fans to get involved and make a difference in their own communities.

Taylor Swift's profound influence has spilled over into the realms of fashion and popular culture, where she has become an icon in her own right. Her sartorial choices have consistently garnered attention and influential praise. From her whimsical and nostalgic aesthetic in her early career to her more sophisticated and bold style in recent years, Swift has effortlessly embraced different personas and pushed style boundaries. Designers have taken notice of her fashion choices, often citing her as an inspiration and collaborating with her on exclusive collections. Her fashion influence has permeated street style and even influenced the runway, making her a tastemaker in the industry.

Moreover, Taylor Swift's transition into acting has served as another testament to her multidimensional talent and enduring influence. Her performances in films such as "Valentine's Day" and "The Giver" showcased her ability to captivate audiences in a different medium, further bolstering her standing as an influential cultural figure. More recently, her role in the film adaptation of the beloved musical "Cats" demonstrated her dedication to taking on challenging roles that showcase her versatility as an artist.

As the years unfold, Taylor Swift's enduring impact will continue to shape the music industry and beyond. Her artistry, authenticity, and dedication to making a difference have paved the way for future generations of musicians and artists to seamlessly blend their creative visions with societal impact. Swift's lasting legacy serves as a guiding light, inspiring others to embrace their unique voices, challenge norms, and use their platforms to effect change on a global scale.